COSTA RICA

ENGLISH

JADINE

Editorial management: Raquel López Varela

Editorial coordination: Antonio Manilla

Layout: Fernando Ampudia

Photographs: David Castañer

Contributors: Hans Venier y Asdrúbal Leiva

Texts: Asdrúbal Leiva C.

SPECIAL EDITION FOR JADINE

© PHOTOGRAPHS: David Castañer
© COLLECTION: EDITORIAL EVEREST, S. A.
Carretera León-La Coruña, km 5 - LEÓN
www.everest.es

ISBN: 84-241-0834-5
Legal deposit: LE. 1068-2005

Printed in Spain – Impreso en España
EDITORIAL EVERGRÁFICAS, S. L.
Carretera León-La Coruña, km 5
LEÓN (Spain)

Customer Information Service: **+34 902 123 400**

Cover: Red-eyed tree frog.
Cover 4: City of San José.
Cover 2/3: Hummingbird/Butterfly.

COSTA RICA

ENGLISH

JADINE

Editorial management: Raquel López Varela

Editorial coordination: Antonio Manilla

Layout: Fernando Ampudia

Photographs: David Castañer

Contributors: Hans Venier y Asdrúbal Leiva

Texts: Asdrúbal Leiva C.

SPECIAL EDITION FOR JADINE

© PHOTOGRAPHS: David Castañer
© COLLECTION: EDITORIAL EVEREST, S. A.
Carretera León-La Coruña, km 5 - LEÓN
www.everest.es

ISBN: 84-241-0834-5
Legal deposit: LE. 1068-2005

Printed in Spain – Impreso en España
EDITORIAL EVERGRÁFICAS, S. L.
Carretera León-La Coruña, km 5
LEÓN (Spain)

Customer Information Service: **+34 902 123 400**

Cover: Red-eyed tree frog.
Cover 4: City of San José.
Cover 2/3: Hummingbird/Butterfly.

NATIONAL PARKS OF COSTA RICA

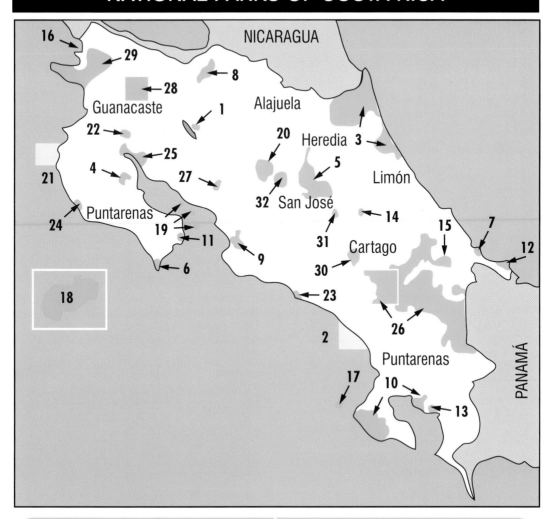

1. Arenal	17. Caño Island
2. Ballena	18. Coco Island
3. Barra del Colorado and Tortuguero	19. Guayabo, Negritos and Pájaros Islands
4. Barra Honda	20. Juan Castro Blanco
5. Braulio Carrillo	21. Las Baulas
6. Cabo Blanco	22. Lomas Barbudal
7. Cahuita	23. Manuel Antonio
8. Caño Negro	24. Ostional
9. Carara	25. Palo Verde
10. Corcovado	26. Parque Inter. la Amistad and Chirripó
11. Curú	27. Peñas Blancas
12. Gandoca-Manzanillo	28. Rincón de la Vieja
13. Golfito	29. Santa Rosa and Guanacaste
14. Guayabo	30. Tapantí
15. Hitoy Cerere	31. Irazú Volcano
16. Bolaños Island	32. Póas Volcano

COSTA RICA, General Information

COSTA RICA

Area: 51,100 km²
(approximately 20,000 sq. miles).
Capital: San José.
Population: 3.900.000.
Currency: Colón.
Borders: Nicaragua to the north and Panama to the south.
Official Language: Spanish.

Costa Rica is a small country located in the southernmost part of Central America. Due to its geographic location and because it is a relatively narrow strip of land between the Caribbean Sea and the Pacific Ocean, a great variety of intertropical flora and fauna can be found here. For this reason, Costa Rica is considered a biological land bridge between North and South America and scientists and experts affirm that Costa Rica boasts some of the most diverse flora and fauna in the world.

Climate
Costa Rica is described as having one of the most pleasant year-round climates to be found anywhere –never too hot or too cold– a temperate climate throughout the country.

The average annual temperature is about 30°C (86°F) along the coasts and 17°C (63°F) in the interior of the country where San José, the capital, is located. Temperatures average 24°C (75°F) during the entire year. Seasons are not well defined in this country, although two main seasons are usually identified. The "green" season runs from May to November with frequent rainfall across the entire country and the dry season is from December to April. This is the season preferred by vacationers and tourists.

The Area
The total area of Costa Rica is just a little over 51,000 km² (approximately 20,000 square miles). Each of the 7 provinces (San José, Alajuela, Cartago, Heredia, Guanacaste, Puntarenas and Limón) has a great variety of attractions, which makes them all well worth the visit.
Along the extensive coastlines, bathed on the west by the Pacific Ocean and on the east by the Caribbean, there are innumerable beaches surrounded by impressive natural beauty which will satisfy any taste.

Population
Today this small country is considered quite cosmopolitan. Its natural attributes, pleasant climate, and peaceful environment have made it a

popular place for many foreigners from many different parts of the world. Every year more than 1,000,000 tourists come to Costa Rica seeking a destination where nature is the main attraction.

Nature
Undoubtedly, the main attraction in Costa Rica is the biological diversity of nature at its best. It is indeed astounding to note that almost 6% of all earth's species have taken up residence in this tropical country that accounts for only 0.03% of the total surface area of the planet. 25% of the country's territory has been reserved for its many national parks which offer many options to tourists who want to enjoy its natural wonders and its beaches in a truly impressive scenic landscape.

Central Avenue. San José, Costa Rica.
Located in the heart of the country, in a valley surrounded by green mountains and impressive volcanoes, San José has been the cosmopolitan capital of Costa Rica since 1823.

The development of the city of San José started in the mid-XIX century with the beginning of coffee exportation to Europe. The "Josefinos" (name given to people from San José) of that time never imagined that this adventure would change their lives and those of their children, bringing them economic growth and cultural superiority in comparison with people of neighboring countries. In that era, many parents were able to send their children to study in Europe, the National Theater was built, San José became one of the first cities in the world to have electric street lights, and free, compulsory public education was instated.

The modern "Josefino" now enjoys strolling on Central Avenue: shopping, resting, and chatting with friends at "Plaza de la Cultura," which is adorned with the beautiful architecture of the National Theater.

The National Theater.

The National Theater.
This beautiful neoclassic-style theater was inaugurated in 1897, with the presentation of the play Fausto, after having been built with funds wrought from coffee exportation. To this day, coffee continues to be the main source of Costa Rica's income. With four levels and excellent acoustics, this theater is decorated with fine wood from the region and the best imported marble. Currently it is still the pride and joy of Costa Ricans and continues to host the country's most select cultural events.

Handicrafts.

Wheel of a typical oxcart.

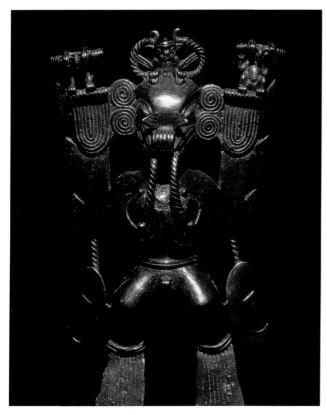

Gold Museum. San José.

Jade Museum. San José.

Guaria Morada (*Guarianthe Skinneri*).
This orchid, Costa Rica's national flower, adorns the fences and tile-roofs of old homes when it blooms in March and December. It may be seen in all its splendor on the 37 acres (15 hectares) of the Lankester Garden in Cartago, alongside hundreds of other species of orchids native to Costa Rica.

12

"Gold Dust".
At the beginning of the 19th century, Costa Rica was already cultivating coffee in the central part of the country and was starting to export it to Europe.

Irazú Volcano.
This volcano rises to a height of 3,432 (11,260 ft.) meters above sea level. The crater can be reached via paved highway from the city of Cartago, 20 miles away.

Basilica of Our Lady of Angels.
Traditionally, hundreds of thousands of pilgrims visit each August 2 to give thanks to the Virgin de los Angeles for favors conceded. The province of Cartago was founded by Juan Vázquez de Coronado in 1563 and is considered the first city in Costa Rica.
In colonial times, when the country belonged to Spain, Cartago was the capital. The declaration of independence from Spain arrived in this province via mail from Guatemala en 1821; two years later, the capital was transferred to San José.

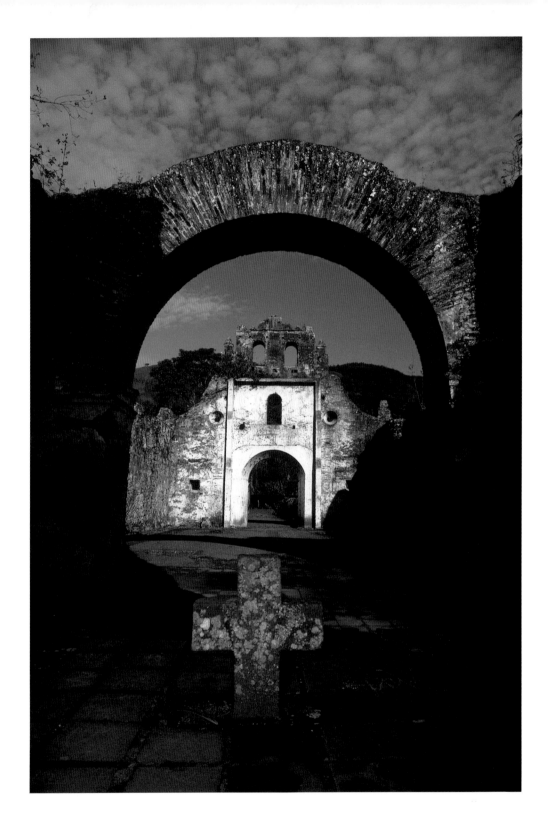

Ujarrás Ruins. Cartago.

Cartago still harbors traces of the colonial era, namely the Ujarrás Ruins and the Church of Orosí. These are currently tourist attractions as is the impressive Irazú Volcano which boasts an enormous and easily-accessible crater. The Byzantine-style Basilica of Our Lady of Los Angeles, built in honor of the Virgin Mary, patron saint of Costa Rica, also known as "La Negrita," is another tourist favorite.

San José Church of Orosí. Cartago.

This church, the most representative example of colonial architecture in the Cartago area, is extremely well-preserved. The Museum of Religious Arts, next door to the church, houses an interesting collection of antiquities and is located on the site of an old Franciscan monastery.

Peach Palm.

The fruit of a common palm variety found mainly on the Atlantic slopes. Used to prepare typical Costa Rican dishes.

Chirripó National Park.
Nestled in the Talamanca Mountain Range, about a 150 km (93 miles) south of San José, the Chirripó National Park covers an extension of 43,700 hectares (108,000 acres). This park is home to the highest peak (also called Chirripó) in Costa Rica. From the foot of its 3,820 mts (12,500 ft), awe-striking vistas of flatlands and marsh may be observed. This Park was declared a World Heritage site by the United Nations in 1983.

Chirripó National Park.

Corcovado National Park.

Located on the Osa Peninsula, which is found in Costa Rica's southern Pacific region, this park possesses the greatest expanse of lowland rainforest in Costa Rica and covers 40,000 hectares (100,000 acres). Corcovado also boasts the largest scarlet macaw population in the country. Furthermore, you may also view other important species such as harpy eagles and tapirs. It is also home to the largest jaguar population in the country.

Sirena Beach.
Corcovado
National Park. ➤

Manuel Antonio National Park.
The park is 105 miles from San José. Its majestic scenery includes beautiful beaches, among the most popular in the nation, and spectacular tropical rainforests. These attributes have made this park a favorite with the tourists.

Manuel Antonio's main attraction is the presence of both beach and forest and its extensive biodiversity. Squirrel monkeys, sloths of several species, mantled howler monkeys and white-faced capuchin monkeys can be easily spotted in its forest. These species can be observed a few meters from the beach or along the forest trails.

White-faced capuchin monkey.

Poás Volcano National Park.
Situated in the Central Volcanic Mountain Range, Poás Volcano National Park is one of the most-frequented tourist attractions. Its main crater has a diameter of nearly 1.5 kilometers (1 mile) and reaches an almost 300 meter (1,000 ft) depth, allowing for an impressive view.
Within the thick forest that surrounds the volcano, many trails are accessible to tourists. Here the hiker can breathe fresh mountain air, enjoy the forest's many springs, observe a great variety of birds (including the Quetzal, the most spectacular and colorful bird in the American tropics) and, of course, marvel at the impressive landscapes.

San Gerardo de Dota.
Heading toward southern Costa Rica on the Inter-American highway, the tourist comes across San Gerardo de Dota , a secluded area of cloud forest, at the foot of the Talamanca Mountain Range. Its main attractions are: enjoying the crystal clear waters of Savegre River, hiking through dense forests filled with bromelias, and watching the quetzal birds which are easily seen as they feed in the lush branches of the forest trees.

Savegre River. ➤

Jacó Beach. Puntarenas.
This is the ideal place for surf and beach lovers alike. Jacó offers a number of recreational options. You may rent a bike to explore the nearby tourist sites, take surfing lessons, or enjoy the nightlife of the many bars and discos, to mention a few. However, surfing is the number-one activity in the area and the favorite spot is nearby Playa Hermosa, a paradise for any surfer.

Jacó Beach. Puntarenas.

The city of Puntarenas in the Central Pacific region.

City of Puntarenas.

Golden rain tree. Guanacaste. ➤➤

Guanacaste.

This province is located in the northwestern region of the country. Its generally dry tropical climate allows the visitor the opportunity to enjoy the sun practically all year long. The name of the province is derived from the luxuriant Guanacaste tree, which is common in the area. Culturally, Guanacaste has its own identity, embodied in the "Sabanero" (the Costa Rican equivalent to a cowboy) and their lively folkloric music. Guanacaste is covered mainly by plains which stretch towards the western part of the mountain range that bears the same name. These mountains form part of the so-called Central American Andes. Important volcanoes are found in this range: namely, the volcanoes El Rincón de la Vieja and Arenal, which are both popular tourist attractions because of their continual volcanic activity. However, Guanacaste's numerous beaches are its most noteworthy attraction. Located primarily on the Nicoya Peninsula and the Papagayo Golf, they are favorites with both tourists and nationals.

Santa Cruz. Guanacaste.

Guiones Beach. Guanacaste.

Howler monkey. ➤

Cañas Catholic
Church. Guanacaste.

Nosara Beach. Guanacaste.

Santa Marta.Guanacaste.

Iguana. ➤

Tamarindo Beach. Guanacaste.

42 ◄◄ Blanca Beach. Montezuma.

Gulf of Nicoya. Puntarenas.

Montezuma. Puntarenas.

Grande Beach. Guanacaste.

Creb.

Monteverde Cloud Forest Biological Reserve.
Found in the Tilarán Mountain Range, the Cloud Forest Reserve offers a wide diversity of plants and animals, home to 2,500 species of plants, 500 species of butterflies and more than 400 species of birds, among which the Quetzal is frequently seen. Monteverde is definitely a "must see" for the ecological tourist and bird and butterfly watcher.

Arenal Volcano. Alajuela.
This cone-shaped volcano has been erupting continually since 1968. These intense eruptions can be seen from a distance, especially at night from one of the many lookout points.

Morpho butterfly.

Celeste River. Alajuela.

Butterfly (Nymphalidae).

Rincón de la Vieja National Park.
Located in the Guanacaste Volcanic Range. There is a great deal of volcanic activity
near the sites of Las Pailas and La Hornilla as well as numerous hot springs.

The Bananito River Basin. Limón.

The Costa Rican Caribbean Coast.
Upon reaching Limón, the visitor immediately perceives the Caribbean atmosphere reflected in its people, food, architecture and customs. Much of this area has been set aside for attractive national parks such as: Tortuguero, Cahuita, Chirripó, Amistad and Braulio Carrillo.

Manzanillo. Limón.

Limón Carnival.

Besides coconut groves, tropical rainforests, and miles of sandy beach and crystal-clear water, the Caribbean plains are known for their white-water rivers, such as the Pacuare and the Reventazón, which are ideal for Class III and IV rafting.

The month of October is filled with festivities as Limón celebrates its Carnival. People take to the street with music, dances and bands, all to the Caribbean beat.

Rafting on the Pacuare River. Limón.

Manzanillo Beach. Limón.

54

Cahuita National Park. Port Vargas.
Located on the Caribbean Cost, this part of the park is surrounded by a coral reef that is host to incredibly diverse marine life.

Punta Mona Beach. Limón.

Cahuita Beach. Limón. ➤➤

Tortuguero National Park. Limón.
One would think that he or she is in the Amazon while sailing on the calm waters of the canals of this park. Within its exuberant vegetation, multicolored parrots, monkeys, birds, crocodiles, and turtles may be readily observed. The beaches of Tortuguero are famous because they are one of the chief American nesting grounds for the leatherback sea turtle. The turtles arrive here by the hundreds every year. Sailing north of Tortuguero, one encounters the National Wildlife Refuge, Barra Del Colorado, which borders Nicaragua. This Refuge provides a sanctuary for the tropical gar fish, Atractosteus tropicus, considered to be a living fossil, the endangered tapir, crocodiles and caymans.

Basilisk.

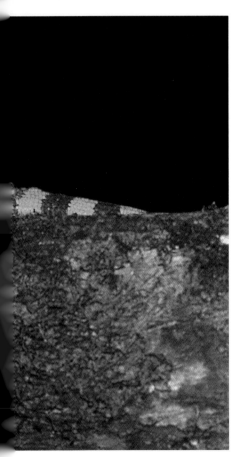

Tropical flower.

Tropical flower.

A giant leatherback.
Known as the largest sea turtle in the word, lays its eggs.

Rufescent (lineated) tiger heron.

Jacana.

Tortuguero Nacional Park. Limón.

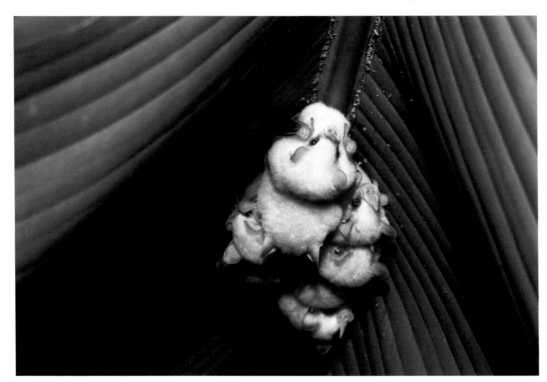

Albino bats.

Anhinga.

Tortuguero Canals. Limón.

Cocoa fruit.